FLOWER FAIRY STORY-BOOKS

THE ALMOND BLOSSOM FAIRY

Fay Marden

Illustrated by Beverlie Manson

Based on The Flower Fairies created by Cicely M Barker

Blackie

In a garden not far from where you live, there are fairies working, busy as bees.

Fairies? What fairies?

The flower fairies, of course: the most enchanting little creatures you have ever seen – or have *never* seen – for they are such timid folk, they hide away.

Every tree and flower belongs to a flower fairy or an elf. It is their job to look after all the lovely things growing in the world. Did you know that?

No? Then I have so many exciting stories to tell you. Listen and I will tell you a story about the Almond Blossom Fairy.

Almond Blossom loved her tree but, I am sorry to tell you, she loved it so much that she had no time for anything or anyone else. Almond Blossom thought her tree was very special and much better than all the other trees or flowers in the garden.

In springtime, she spent all day skipping from branch to branch, dusting each cluster of delicate pink blossoms. She was so very proud of them and took great care to protect them from icy winds in March or from April showers.

When she wasn't dusting petals, Almond Blossom was busy polishing the boughs – polishing even the tiniest twigs, so that they looked as shiny as new pins. No wonder she had no time to play or be friends with any of the other flower fairies!

One day, the Fuchsia Fairy came visiting. She had been watching Almond Blossom hard at work and had brought her a nutful of fresh dewdrops to drink.

But, oh dear! Almond Blossom was not at all pleased.

'Be careful!' she cried, when Fuchsia fluttered down and settled on a bough. 'I'm sure your wings are covered with dust and cobwebs from the garden. You will make my tree so dirty. Be off with you!'

Poor Fuchsia was hurt by these unkind words. With a whirr of her dainty wings, she flew away.

The flower fairies were most upset when Fuchsia told
them her story. 'How unfriendly,' said the Guelder
Rose Fairy. 'After all, we love and care for our flowers,
too, but I hope we are not so fussy as Almond
Blossom.'

   'She's much too bossy,' said a pixie who had once
had his ears boxed by Almond Blossom for swinging on
her boughs. 'Bossy Blossy, that's what I call her!'

   'We must try to make her understand that she is not
quite so special,' croaked an old green frog. 'Then
perhaps she will be more friendly.'

'Yes, but how?' asked Fuchsia. 'Almond Blossom is always so busy spring-cleaning, she never has time to come down to the garden.'

'Let's have a meeting tonight,' suggested the Sweet Pea Fairy. 'When we have all finished our work, we could gather in the Dell and think of a plan.'

'What a good idea. Clever Sweet Pea,' chorused all the little creatures.

And they ran through the garden to tell their friends.

All this while, Almond Blossom had been fussing around her tree. She carefully tended each new tiny bud and waved away insects that came too near. She spent hours painting each pale pink petal, with the finest paintbrush you have ever seen.

And I am sorry to say that she also chased away the birds – even the little bluetits, who perched on her branches and were so pretty to watch.

'Shoo!' she scolded. 'You birds make such a mess!'

The birds were very startled to be treated in this way. All the other fairies were so friendly and polite.

That night, when the silver moon was high, the fairy folk, birds and woodland creatures gathered in the Fairy Dell. It was an enchanted place – a woody hollow, with sloping banks of soft, green moss, nestling beneath an oak tree. Toadstools grew in plenty and the sweet scent of bluebells filled the air.

Soon the Dell was full of little folk. Granny Spider sat spinning her web. Small, sleepy birds kept themselves awake by chattering in the bushes round about, while the flower fairies formed a circle, seated on cushions of moss.

Of course, the Almond Blossom Fairy was not there. She was alone in her tree, curled up in a bed of pink blossom, singing a lullaby:

'Gentle moonbeams pale and bright,
Shine upon my boughs tonight.
Nothing in the world could be,
Lovelier than my almond tree!'

'Listen,' whispered all the little folk in the Dell, for
Almond Blossom's voice could be heard far and wide.
    'Oh dear,' sighed Sweet Pea. 'We must show
Almond Blossom that we are all special in our own way
and we must live and work together.'

'But how?' asked the Lavender Fairy. Then, Guelder
Rose stood in the middle of the fairy ring and spoke.
	'Listen, I have an idea . . .' she whispered, 'let me
explain. . .'
	Everyone thought it was a wonderful plan. They
would try it the very next day. Then, before they went
to bed that night, with the stars twinkling overhead, the
flower fairies sipped cowslip wine and ate honey cakes
bought from the Busy Bee shop.

The next day, Almond Blossom woke feeling
sulky. She had heard the merry laughter of the meeting
in the Dell and secretly wished she had been invited.

She looked down from her tree and caught sight of
one small pixie, playing below. She gave him such a
cross look that he gave a squeak of alarm and scuttled
off to his mother.

The flower fairies were much too excited to work that day. They were all waiting for a signal from Guelder Rose, a signal that meant they could put their plan into action.

Guelder Rose was floating gently round the almond tree, taking care not to let Almond Blossom see her. Granny Spider was swinging on a very long thread which she had hooked on to a wide, spreading branch.

How quickly she worked!

She was spinning a web. Spinning and spinning, thread after thread until . . . it was quite large enough to hold . . . what do you think? A fairy!

Now, while Granny Spider had been spinning below, Almond Blossom had been busy at the top of her tree, counting all the new leaves.

'Six here. Two there. Four on that branch . . . ten on this!'

Almond Blossom was so busy counting, she didn't see Guelder Rose wave her arms from side to side. For that was the signal for her plan to begin!

Lavender, Sweet Pea and Fuchsia flew up from the
garden and unhooked Granny Spider's web. Then,
quiet as a whisper, they took it to the top of the tree and,
before Almond Blossom knew what was happening,
they had thrown the web right over her.

Poor Almond Blossom! She was completely taken
by surprise.

'What are you doing?' she cried. 'Set me free at
once!'

'We are taking you down to the garden,' said the
flower fairies, who had cradled her gently in the web,
for they did not wish to hurt her.

Almond Blossom was as cross as could be but she
could not escape those tangled threads.

Then, light as thistledown, Lavender, Sweet Pea
and Fuchsia took hold of the cradle and flew down.
They set Almond Blossom on a mossy bank and
Fuchsia made sure that she was quite comfortable, even
though she was still held fast in the spider's web.

'Oh, how horrid this is!' complained Almond Blossom, as she wriggled and squirmed. 'How dirty the ground is! Why are you doing this to me?'

Then Guelder Rose flew down beside her and explained.

'Hush now,' she said. 'Look around you, listen and learn.'

Almond Blossom stopped wriggling and looked around the garden. It was as if she were seeing it for the first time.

She looked at the grass – each blade so tall and slender and green. She noticed so many different flowers, their colours and soft scents. There were narcissi growing beneath her own dear tree which she had never seen before. How pretty they were!

Almond Blossom listened to the merry chatter of the flower fairies busy about their work. How cheerful they were, singing and calling to one another. Everyone was as busy as a bee but the work seemed so much fun!

Almond Blossom felt tears coming to her eyes. How unkindly she had treated them all. How ashamed she felt, and how she longed to have friends, for now she saw how lonely and unhappy she had been!

Poor dear creature! She cried and cried and was so very sorry.

'There, there,' soothed Sweet Pea. 'Don't cry so. We don't want you to be sad.'

'But we *do* want you to be good and kind,' said Guelder Rose, 'and to remember that we are all as important as each other.'

'And above all,' said Lavender, 'we want you to be our friend!'

'You have been very kind,' sobbed Almond Blossom. 'I am truly sorry that I have been so horrid to you all.'

'Come,' said Granny Spider, who had been climbing down to the ground on one of her long threads. 'Let me undo my web and set you free.'

Then how the fairies crowded round her, laughing and talking. The elves and pixies joined in the fun and played catch-as-catch-can with the woodmice and voles, until Almond Blossom laughed so much, her sides ached.

'You may all come and visit my tree as often as you wish,' said Almond Blossom, as she sipped dandelion tea from an acorn cup.

'We will,' chorused the fairy folk, as they danced in a ring around her.

And as far as I know, they did.

The Flower Fairies copyright © The Estate of Cicely M Barker
1923, 1925, 1926, 1934, 1940, 1944, 1948
Text copyright © Fay Marden 1986
Illustrations copyright © Blackie and Son Ltd 1986

First published 1986 by
Blackie and Son Ltd
7 Leicester Place, London WC2H 7BP

British Library Cataloguing in Publication Data
Marden, Fay
    The almond blossom fairy.—(Flower fairies
    story books)
    I. Title   II. Beverlie Manson   III. Barker,
    Cicely Mary   IV. Series
    823'.914[J]   PZ7

    ISBN 0-216-91979-7

Printed in Great Britain by
Holmes McDougall Limited, Edinburgh